THE ROLLING STONES

AFTERMATH

ALBUM NOTES

Release Date: July, 1966

Top Chart Position: No. 2, reached August 13, 1966

Standout Tracks: "Paint It, Black," "Under My Thumb" and "Lady Jane"

Significance: The first Rolling Stones album to feature all-original material; incorporated the influence of psychedelia and folk-rock; showcased the band's multi-instrumental diversity (sitar, vibraphone, dulcimer, marimba, harpsichord); signaled the Stones' transition from blues-based rock and roll band to inventive, groundbreaking artists.

Milestone: The first album composed entirely by the songwriting team of Mick Jagger and Keith Richards.

ISBN-10: 0-7390-4163-0
ISBN-13: 978-0-7390-4163-5

FOREWORD

Aftermath was truly a watershed album for the Rolling Stones. After "Satisfaction" had established the band as a massive force to be reckoned with, anticipation was huge for the new album that was released in July, 1966. It was the Stones' sixth U.S. studio album and the first that was comprised entirely of songs written by Mick Jagger and Keith Richards. While this may have seemed of small significance at the time, these days when one thinks of the preeminent songwriting teams of the second half of the 20th century, Jagger and Richards usually spring right to mind. *Aftermath* is where this kind of thinking was codified.

The album had something of a dark aura but was hardly lugubrious in tone; it was cutting but never mopey. Beyond Mick and Keith's songs, which have achieved a kind of immortality of their own, the album is noteworthy for Brian Jones's laudable efforts to give the band instrumental diversity while keeping it all very rock and roll. With *Aftermath*, the band had grown from an R&B beat band to an inventive, artistic groundbreaking force in rock, pop and whatever else you choose to call it.

The album is filled with idiosyncratic songs that seem magically atmospheric, underscored by "Paint It, Black" which was a No.1 single despite (or, perhaps, because of) its dirge-like urgency. There's the snarling and unapologetic "Under My Thumb," the Elizabethan balladry of "Lady Jane," counterbalanced by the disparaging "Stupid Girl," and not forgetting the vocal hall of mirrors in the double-wide album closer "Going Home." Every song is singular including the courtly "I Am Waiting," the R&B swagger of "It's Not Easy," the ass-kicking "High and Dry," the jet-age diary "Flight 505," the soul-inflected "Think," and "Doncha Bother Me"—an uncharacteristic jingly-jangly outing in the mode of Bob Dylan's "Rainy Day Women #12 and 35," without the giggles.

The band's basic two-guitar, bass and drums format was augmented on selected tracks with bits of exotica from sitars and marimbas, Renaissance echoes from the dulcimer and harpsichord, along with piano and organ. Charlie, Bill, Brian, Keith and Mick were joined for the effort by Jack Nitzsche and Ian Stewart, with Andrew Loog Oldham producing once more.

The *Aftermath* recording sessions took place at RCA Studios on Sunset Boulevard in Hollywood over the course of only two days in December, 1965. Those two days, spent in the studio over 40 years ago, established the band as a vortex of creative energy and innovation. And that's the way it's been ever since.

THE ROLLING STONES

AFTERMATH

CONTENTS

PAINT IT, BLACK

6

Outro:

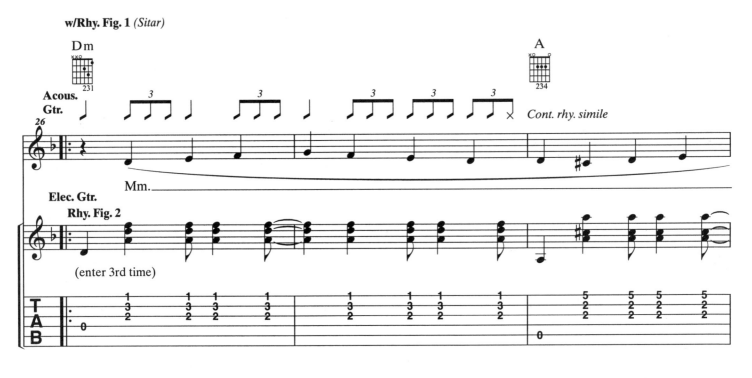

Verse 3:
I look inside myself and see my heart is black.
I see my red door I must have it painted black.

Bridge 3:
Maybe then I'll fade away and not have to face the facts.
It's not easy facing up when your whole world is black.

Verse 4:
No more will my green sea go turn a deeper blue.
I could not foresee this thing happening to you.

Bridge 4:
If I look hard enough into the setting sun,
My love will laugh with me before the mornin' comes.
(To Verse 5:)

STUPID GIRL

Moderately ♩ = 132

Intro:

Words and Music by
MICK JAGGER and KEITH RICHARDS

10

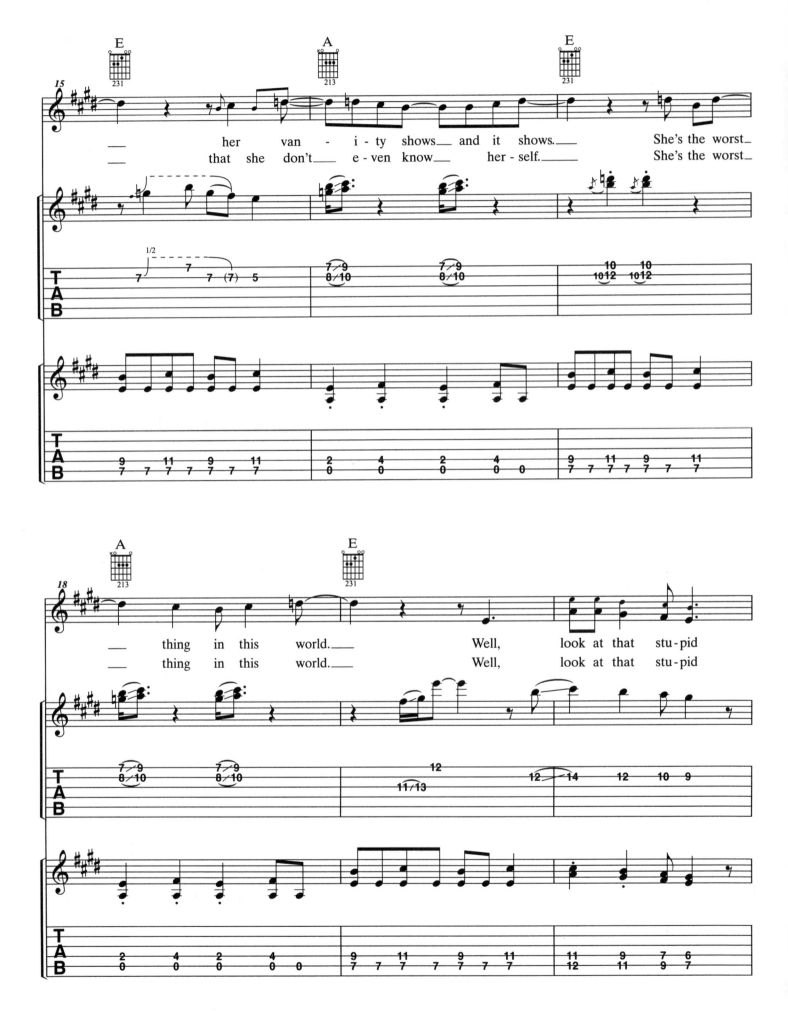

Stupid Girl - 8 - 3
25776

12

I've   tried   and   tried,_____   but it

D.S. 𝄋 al Coda

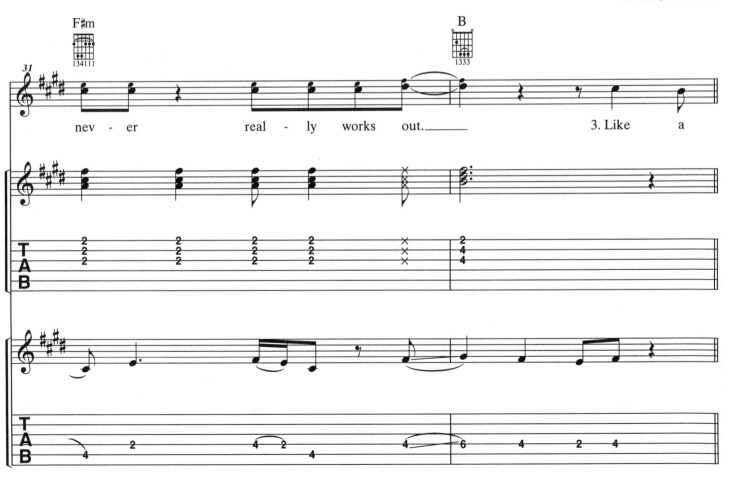

nev - er   real - ly   works   out._____   3. Like   a

14

Stupid Girl - 8 - 7
25776

Verse 3:
Like a lady in waiting to a virgin queen.
Look at that stupid girl.
She bitches 'bout things that she's never seen.
Look at that stupid girl.
It doesn't matter if she dyes her hair,
Or the color of the shoes she wears.
She's the worst thing in the world.
Well, look at that stupid girl.
(To Guitar Solo:)

LADY JANE

Words and Music by
MICK JAGGER and KEITH RICHARDS

Moderately ♩ = 104

Intro:

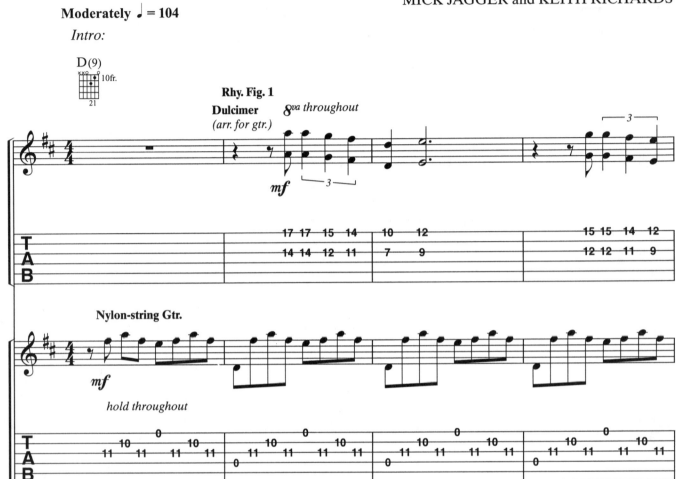

𝄋 *Verse:*

w/Rhy. Fig. 1 *(Dulcimer)*

UNDER MY THUMB

Moderately ♩ = 126

Words and Music by
MICK JAGGER and KEITH RICHARDS

Outro:

Repeat and fade

Verse 3:
Under my thumb, is a Siamese cat of a girl.
Under my thumb, she's the sweetest, *hmmm,* pet in the world.

Chorus 3:
It's down to me;
The way she talks when she's spoken to.
Down to me, the change has come, she's under my thumb.
Ah, oh, take it easy.

Verse 4:
Under my thumb, her eyes are just kept to herself.
Under my thumb, well, I, I can still look at someone else.

Chorus 5:
It's down to me, oh, that's what I said.
The way she talks when she's spoken to.
Down to me, the change has come, she's under my thumb.
Say, it's alright.

DONCHA BOTHER ME

Words and Music by
MICK JAGGER and KEITH RICHARDS

Don-cha   fol - low.

Cont. in slashes

32

Don-cha   fol-low.

Outro:

Repeat ad lib. and fade

Doncha Bother Me - 6 - 6
25776

THINK

Words and Music by
MICK JAGGER and KEITH RICHARDS

Moderately ♩ = 126

34

Cont. in slashes

Lyrics:
You should just re-trace your steps___ and think back,___ back, a
Here's an-oth-er piece of my___ mind: Think back,___ back, a
You're get-ting old be-fore your time,___ and think back,___ back, a

38

Think - 12 - 6
25776

think back, ba - by. Think, think, back a bit, girl.___

Think - 12 - 7
25776

Think, think, think back, ba - by. Tell me whose fault was that,

*Vocal on repeat only.

44

Repeat and fade

think.____

I said,

Think - 12 - 12
25776

FLIGHT 505

Words and Music by
MICK JAGGER and KEITH RICHARDS

48

Flight 505 - 7 - 4
25776

D.S. 𝄋 al Coda

3. Well,

Coda

Al - right.____

Elec. Gtr. 2

Elec. Gtr. 1

Instrumental:

Elec. Gtrs. 1 & 2 cont. verse fig. simile

He put___

HIGH AND DRY

*Tune down 1 whole step:

⑥ = D ③ = F

⑤ = G ② = A

④ = C ① = D

Words and Music by
MICK JAGGER and KEITH RICHARDS

Moderately fast country two-beat ♩ = 116

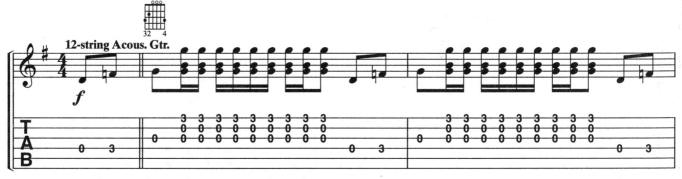

12-string Acous. Gtr.

*Recording sounds one whole step lower than written.

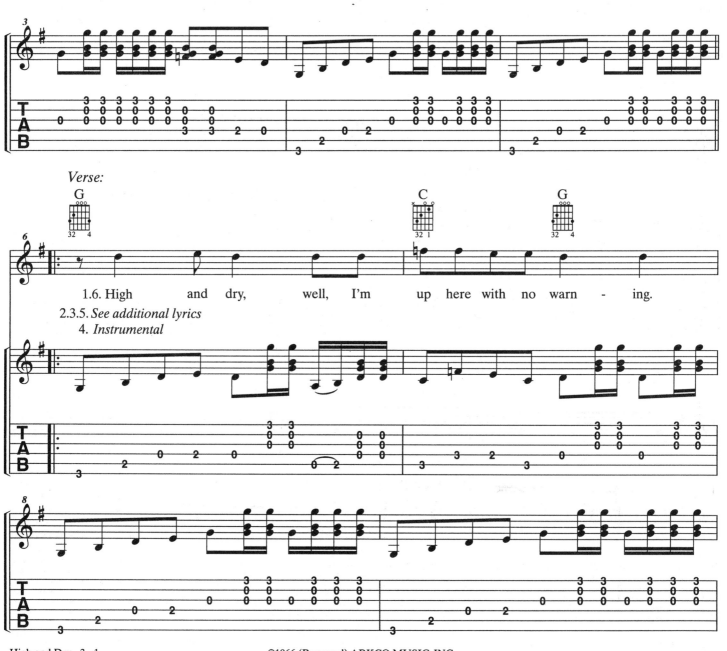

Verse:

1.6. High and dry, well, I'm up here with no warn - ing.

2.3.5. *See additional lyrics*
4. *Instrumental*

High and dry, well, I could - n't get a word in.

High and dry, oh, what a way to go. She

left me stand - ing here just high and dry.

Verse 2:
One minute I was up there, standing by her side.
The next, I was down there, left out of the ridin'.
High and dry, oh, what a way to go.
She left me standing here just high and dry.

Verse 3:
Anything I wished for, I only had to ask her.
I think she found out it was the money I was after.
High and dry, oh, what a wierd let down.
She left me standing here just high and dry.
(To Verse 4: Instrumental)

Verse 5:
It's lucky that I didn't have any love towards her.
Next time I'll make sure that the girl will be much poorer.
High and dry, oh, what a way to go.
She left me standing here just high and dry.
Well, she left me standing here just high and dry.
Well, she left me standing here just high and dry.

IT'S NOT EASY

Words and Music by
MICK JAGGER and KEITH RICHARDS

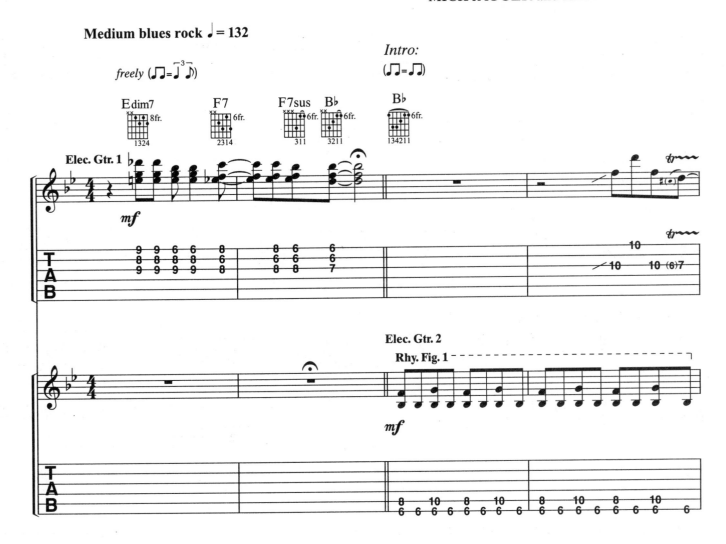

56

It's Not Easy - 7 - 2
25776

59

It's Not Easy - 7 - 5
25776

I AM WAITING

Words and Music by
MICK JAGGER and KEITH RICHARDS

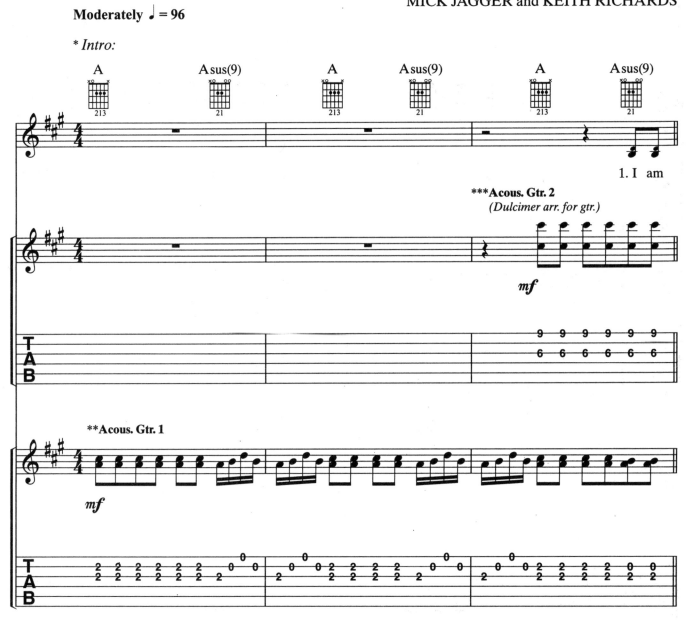

**Acous. Gtr. 1 w/capo III, ① = D.
TAB numbers and chord frames relative to capo and ① = D.

***Acous. Gtr. 2 w/capo III, standard tuning.
TAB numbers relative to capo.

*Recording sounds 1 1/2 steps higher than written.

64

I Am Waiting - 6 - 3
25776

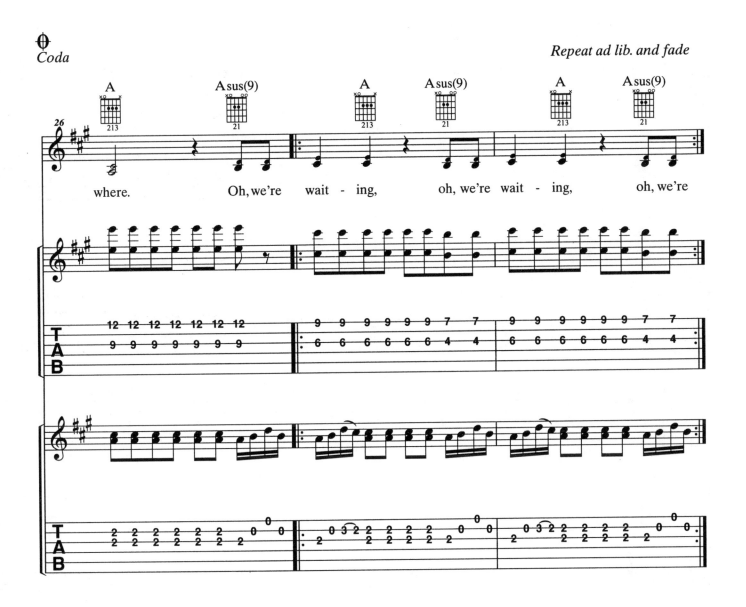

Coda

where. Oh, we're wait - ing, oh, we're wait - ing, oh, we're

Verse 3:
Slow or fast, slow or fast, oh yeah, oh yeah.
End at last, end at last, oh yeah, oh yeah.
Waiting for someone to come out of somewhere.
Waiting for someone to come out of somewhere.
(To Bridge 2:)

Verse 4:
Oh, we're waiting, oh we're waiting, oh yeah, oh yeah.
Oh, we're waiting, oh we're waiting, oh yeah, oh yeah.
Waiting for someone to come out of somewhere.
Waiting for someone to come out of somewhere.
(To Coda)

GOING HOME

70

72

I'm go-ing

76

Going Home - 12 - 9
25776

Gotta, gotta, gotta, gotta, gotta, see my baby.

She'll make me feel so good.___

She'll make me feel alright, al-right, al-right, al-right, al-right, al-right. Yes, she does___ in the middle of the night.

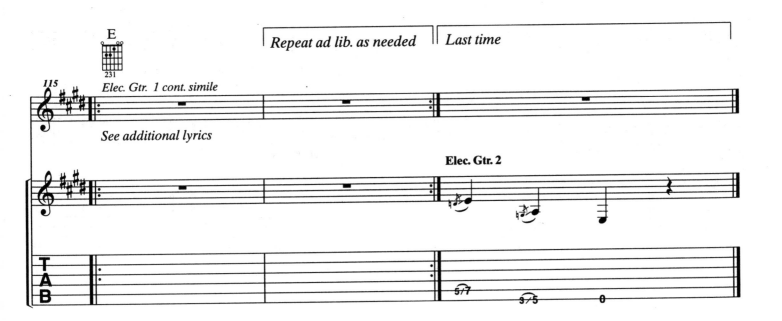

Lyrics for ad lib.
So good, so tight.
Feel alright, come on, baby.
I'm gonna get home, babe.
I feel alright.
I'm lookin' for my baby.
I'm gonna go in the early morning.
I'm gonna catch that plane.
Now it won't be long, I say.
Listen to me.
Long time since I've seen my baby.
Yes, it is.
It's such a long, long time.
Yes, it is, I feel alright.
I'm gonna see my baby, one more time.
I get home, I gotta get home.
I wanna see my darling.
I wanna make sweet, sweet love
In the middle of the night,
Early in the morning,
In the midnight hour.
She'll make me feel so good.
She'll make me feel alright.

When she touch my hands,
And that's all I gotta say.
'Cause I'm gonna pack my bags.
I wanna see you, baby,
See your face,
Your pretty little smile,
Your pretty clothes.
Hear you talk.
Come on.
I'm comin' home.
I'll see my baby.
I'm going home.
I'm gettin' out .
To see your face
Makin' love to you, baby.
Yes, it makes me feel so good inside.
I feel so good inside.
Touch me one more time.
Come on, little girl.
You may look sweet.
But I know you ain't.
I know you ain't.

GUITAR TAB GLOSSARY **

TABLATURE EXPLANATION

READING TABLATURE: Tablature illustrates the six strings of the guitar. Notes and chords are indicated by the placement of fret numbers on a given string(s).

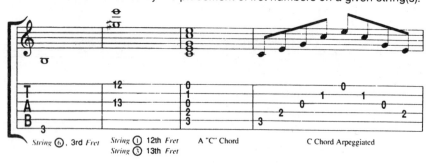

String ⑥ , 3rd Fret   String ① 12th Fret   A "C" Chord   C Chord Arpeggiated
String ③ 13th Fret

BENDING NOTES

HALF STEP: Play the note and bend string one half step.*

WHOLE STEP: Play the note and bend string one whole step.

PREBEND AND RELEASE: Bend the string, play it, then release to the original note.

RHYTHM SLASHES

G   C

STRUM INDICA-TIONS: Strum with indicated rhythm.

The chord voicings are found on the first page of the transcription underneath the song title.

INDICATING SINGLE NOTES USING RHYTHM SLASHES: Very often single notes are incorporated into a rhythm part. The note name is indicated above the rhythm slash with a fret number and a string indication.

*A half step is the smallest interval in Western music; it is equal to one fret. A whole step equals two frets.

**By Kenn Chipkin and Aaron Stang

ARTICULATIONS

HAMMER ON: Play lower note, then "hammer on" to higher note with another finger. Only the first note is attacked.

PULL OFF: Play higher note, then "pull off" to lower note with another finger. Only the first note is attacked.

LEGATO SLIDE: Play note and slide to the following note. (Only first note is attacked).

PALM MUTE: The note or notes are muted by the palm of the pick hand by lightly touching the string(s) near the bridge.

ACCENT: Notes or chords are to be played with added emphasis.

DOWN STROKES AND UPSTROKES: Notes or chords are to be played with either a downstroke (⊓ ・) or upstroke (∨) of the pick.

© 1990 Beam Me Up Music
c/o CPP/Belwin, Inc. Miami, Florida 33014